WHY SHOULD I SHARE?

Books in the
WHY SHOULD I? Series:

WHY SHOULD I Protect Nature?   WHY SHOULD I Eat Well?
WHY SHOULD I Recycle?   WHY SHOULD I Help?
WHY SHOULD I Save Water?   WHY SHOULD I Listen?
WHY SHOULD I Save Energy?   WHY SHOULD I Share?

First edition for the United States, its territories and dependencies,
and Canada published in 2005 by Barron's Educational Series, Inc.

First published in Great Britain in 2001 by Hodder Wayland, an imprint
of Hodder Children's Books.
© Copyright 2001 Hodder Wayland
Hodder Children's Books
A division of Hodder Headline Ltd.
338 Euston Road
London NW1 3BH
United Kingdom
Reprinted 2002 and 2004

All inquiries should be addressed to:
Barron's Educational Series, Inc.
250 Wireless Boulevard
Hauppauge, NY 11788
www.barronseduc.com

International Standard Book Number 0-7641-3220-2

Library of Congress Catalog Card Number 2004113857

Printed in China
9 8 7 6 5 4 3 2 1

WHY SHOULD I SHARE?

Written by Claire Llewellyn

Illustrated by Mike Gordon

BARRON'S

Mom was angry with me this morning.
It was all about me not sharing.

4

Then I wouldn't share the yo-yo ...

Mom said sharing is a kind thing to do. It shows that you are thinking about other people, and not just about yourse

8

She said, "What do you think will happen if you don't share your toys?"

"And guess what will happen if you don't share snacks?"

11

"Your friends won't like you anymore.

"And what do you think will happen if you're mean to Jack and won't let him play with the yo-yo?"

"I'll take it away, and then nobody will have any fun."

14

Humph!
I was so mad I went next door
to see the twins.

Kay and Kathy are my best friends.
They told me they had grown up
sharing.

They said sharing made
things more fun.

The three of us played together
all afternoon.

And I began to see what
they meant.

haring was more fun,
nd friendlier, too.

Sharing can make
things a whole lot better.
I mean, what's the point of
having a brand-new frisbee

you don't
hare it with a friend?

And, although it's great to
have your own special pet,

it's twice as good to
share him with your friends.

Sharing can also be useful. Some people share things now and then.

Others share them all the time.

I thought I could try a bit harder to share.
After lunch, I was listening to my headphones, and Jack was feeling left out.

So I said, "Here, you can listen, too."

Oh, Tim
that's sweet of
you to share.

Sharing is friendly and
makes people happy.
And there's another goo[d]
thing about it, too –
once you learn to
share with others

28

they just might
learn to share
with you!

Notes for parents and teachers

Why Should I?

These books will help young readers to recognize what they like and dislike, what is fair and unfair, and what is right and wrong; to think about themselv learn from their experiences, and recognize what they are good at. Some title in this series will help to teach children how to make simple choices that improve their health and well-being, to maintain personal hygiene, and to lec rules for, and ways of, keeping safe, including basic road safety. Reading the books will help children recognize how their behavior affects other people, to listen to other people, and play and work cooperatively, and that family and friends should care for one another.

About Why Should I Share?

Why Should I Share? is intended to be an enjoyable book that discusses the importance of sharing. Sharing is often a difficult thing for children to do A variety of situations throughout this book explore the ways in which sharir can benefit people.

Sharing is a way of giving. Taking turns with a toy or sharing snacks and equipment encourages children to develop relationships with others. Working and playing together teaches children to cooperate – with their families, their friends, and people at school. It is a way of getting along with others.

Sharing is a way of understanding other people's feelings. Some children find it hard to think of anything outside themselves. Being on the receiving end of someone's generosity (or perhaps selfishness) may help to encourage empathy in children and to develop an understanding and knowledge of themselves as individuals.

ring encourages children to feel good about themselves. Children
uld always be praised for sharing. Positive feedback helps to enhance
ir self-esteem.

ggestions as you read the book with children

book is full of examples when children succeed or fail at sharing. As you
e across each example, it might be useful to stop and discuss it with
dren. Are there some things they find hard to share? What are they?

all like it when people are willing to share with us. Can they think of any
es when this has happened to them? What were the circumstances?

the children about what sharing actually means. Why is sharing important?
them to try to imagine a world where no one shared. Would people be
pier or sadder? Encourage them to think about the fact that they belong to
ous groups and communities, such as their family and school, and that it
uld be impossible for these groups and communities to function without
ring.

also share the environment with every other person and animal in the
rld, and sharing in this case means exercising responsibility.

ggested follow-up activities

n a group task, such as building a model castle, which entails sharing
ipment with other pupils or friends.

ldren could ask their grandparents or another older person how they
red things when they were young. During World War II, people had to
re possessions, such as clothes and food, so there would be enough
jo around. Do they think that people used to share more in those days?

Play a game in which two pirates have to share some found booty. Draw pictures of a treasure chest, jewelry, treasure map, coins, etc. Can the childre share the treasure fairly?

Books to read

Chip's Sharing Day by Linda Derkez and Phoebe Doehring (iPicturebooks, 200

Jungle Jam, The Bear Who Wouldn't Share: A Story About, You Guessed It, Sharing (Fancy Monkey Studios, 2002)

Sharing Secrets by Mary Palmer (Windswept House Publications, 1994)

Stone Soup Tales: Recipes for Sharing by The Children's Cabinet (Favorite Recipes Press, 2003)